Birthday Cakes for kids

Publications International, Ltd.

Favorite Brand Name Recipes at www.fbnr.com

Recipe Development: Dari Carré, ErdaTek, Inc.; Teri Rys-Maki

Photography: Sanders Studios, Inc.
Photographer: Kathy Sanders
Photo Assistant: Scott Olson
Prop Stylist: Kathy Lapin
Food Stylists: Carol Parik, Teri Rys-Maki
Studio Coordinator: Kathy Ores

Pictured on the front cover *(clockwise from top left):* Where's the Fire *(page 86),* Flower Power *(page 32),* Prince the Frog *(page 66)* and Dream Castle *(page 30).*

Pictured on the back cover *(top to bottom):* Catch Some Rays *(page 26),* Peanut *(page 62)* and Slam Dunk *(page 74).*

ISBN: 0-7853-5177-9

Manufactured in China.

8 7 6 5 4 3 2 1

Microwave Cooking: Microwave ovens vary in wattage. Use the cooking times as guidelines and check for doneness before adding more time.

Contents

6

Birthday Cake Basics

Before You Begin

A child's birthday is a wonderful occasion to celebrate and create happy memories that can last a lifetime. There are always bakeries or grocery stores that can provide a cake, but why not make the day extra special with a unique, custom-made—and homemade—birthday cake? Whether your child likes monsters or magic, cars or castles, there's a cake here to please everyone. And doing it yourself is easier than you think! Each recipe in *Birthday Cakes for Kids* has easy-to-follow step-by-step directions and a beautiful photo to help you decorate your cake like a professional. Choose one of our basic cake and frosting recipes on pages 92–93, or use a cake mix and prepared frosting—either way, you'll get great results! For helpful tips, read through the following information before starting.

Special Equipment

The right equipment not only makes cake decorating easier but also gives more professional results. All of the equipment mentioned here is available in stores carrying cake decorating supplies.

• Flexible metal spatulas of various sizes are useful in applying frosting.

Use one with a narrow tip to get into small areas. A large flexible metal spatula makes smoothing the frosting on large flat areas easier.

• Wooden toothpicks and wooden or metal skewers are useful for marking designs and lines on cakes.

• Paste food colors are recommended for coloring the frosting as they do not thin the frosting like liquid colorings, and they create bright, vibrant colors. For more information on coloring frosting, see pages 11–12.

• A pastry bag with several tips is essential for piping decorations. The pastry bag can be a traditional reusable pastry bag (made of canvas or plastic-lined cloth) or a disposable plastic pastry bag. We recommend a few basic decorating tips: several sizes of writing tips (numbers 3, 5, 9 and 12) and a star tip (number 28). A coupler is also helpful to have; this piece is inserted into the pastry bag before filling and makes changing

tips easier. See pages 12–13 for a more information on using a pastry bag and decorating tips.

• Cake boards are made of heavy cardboard and are used for cakes that are too large to fit on a plate or tray. See page 10 for instructions on how to cover cake boards.

Basic Cake Know-How

Cake Mixes vs. Cakes from Scratch

Using a packaged cake mix can save time, but be aware that cakes made from mixes are usually more tender and crumbly than cakes made from scratch. It's a good idea to place the cooled cake in the freezer for 30 to 45 minutes to firm up the cake for easier cutting, frosting and decorating.

The Best Baking Pans

For great cakes, use shiny metal pans or pans with a nonstick finish. Grease and flour *ALL* pans before adding the cake batter, including 13×9-inch pans, so that the cakes can be easily removed from the pans. Even nonstick pans should be lightly greased and floured.

Cakes in All Shapes & Sizes

Some of these recipes require standard 13×9 inch cakes or 9-inch round or square cake layers, while others call for bowl-shaped cakes and cupcakes. To make the more

unusual cakes, prepare the cake recipe of your choice—scratch or mix—and pour the specified amount of batter into the pans. Bowl cakes can be made in any ovenproof glass or metal mixing bowl; they are greased and floured just like regular cake pans. (If you use a glass bowl, reduce the oven temperature by 25°F.) Since a traditional cake mix yields about 5½ cups batter per package, there is often some batter left over after filling the pans according to the recipe directions. We recommend that you pour this extra batter into greased (or paper-lined) muffin cups, as it's always useful to have a few extra cupcakes on hand (especially in a house with kids)!

Testing for Doneness

Always bake cakes at the oven temperature and time specified in the recipe. Test cakes after the shortest time given. A cake is done when a toothpick or wooden skewer inserted into the center comes out clean. It should pull away from the side of the pan and spring back when lightly touched in the center. White and yellow cakes should be lightly browned.

Cooling Cakes

Let cakes cool in the pan on a wire rack for about 10 minutes. Loosen cake edges with a spatula and place the rack, top side down, over the pan. Flip the rack and the pan over together and the cake should drop out onto the rack. If it does not come out, tap the bottom of the pan; the cake should come out easily. Remove the pan. If using a waxed paper liner, carefully peel it off while the cake is still warm. Place a second wire rack over the cake and flip both racks and the cake back over so the cake can cool top side up. Remove the top rack. If a cake is removed from the pan too soon, it may crack and break. If it is allowed to cool too long in the pan, it may stick to the pan. Always cool a cake *completely* before frosting—about 4 hours or more.

Storing Cakes

Cool cakes completely before covering and storing. If using the undecorated cake layers within two days, wrap tightly in foil or plastic wrap and store in a cool place. For longer storage, wrap in heavy-duty foil or place in airtight freezer bags; freeze for up to two months. To thaw, remove the layers from the freezer and let them thaw, unwrapped, at room temperature.

Before Frosting

Trimming Cakes

Trimmed cakes are easier to frost and give more professional results. For best results, use a serrated knife long enough to cut across the top in one stroke. Use a gentle sawing motion as you cut through the cake. The rounded tops of round, square

and rectangular cakes should be trimmed to form a flat surface.

The sides of cakes that are square or rectangular should also be trimmed to make them more even.

Use a soft pastry brush to remove all loose cake crumbs. Brush away crumbs again after cutting the cake.

Cutting Cakes

For cleaner cutting lines and fewer crumbs, freeze the cake for 30 to 45 minutes. (This is especially recommended when using cakes made from mixes.) When cutting each cake design, use the diagrams and photos as a guide and follow the directions carefully. A ruler and toothpicks are helpful to mark designs and act as a guide while cutting.

The shaded areas in the diagrams are unused portions of cake. Carefully position all pieces on a plate, tray or cake board. Connect the pieces with some of the frosting.

Leftover cake scraps can be used in a number of ways. Layer them with pudding or softened ice cream for a wonderful parfait. Serve under fresh berries and fruit as a sweet shortcake or use as the base for a trifle. Or, sprinkle crumbs on top of desserts or sundaes. And, easiest of all, they make a wonderful snack for hungry kids.

Assembling Cakes

Many decorated cakes are too large for standard plates and platters. Use cake boards, cutting boards, cookie sheets or other large flat surfaces. Cake boards can be covered with foil, greaseproof paper, paper doilies or plastic wrap. To cover, cut the foil or paper 1 to 2 inches larger than the board. Center the board on the reverse side of the paper. Cut slashes in the paper almost to the board along any place that is curved. This allows the paper to fit smoothly over the board. Fold the edges over the board and tape into place. If a cake is very large or heavy, two cake boards may be stacked together before covering for additional support.

To keep the plate or covered cake board clean, tuck strips of waxed paper underneath the assembled cake before frosting. When decorating is complete, carefully slide out the strips and touch up the frosting as needed.

The Frosting Story

Frosting Consistency

The proper frosting consistency is the secret to successful decorating. Buttercream Frosting (page 92) should hold its shape when scooped with a spatula.

If the frosting is too soft because the kitchen is warm, try refrigerating the frosting for about 15 minutes and keep it chilled while you work. If the frosting is too soft because liquid coloring was used or too much milk was added, beat in some additional sifted powdered sugar. If the frosting is too stiff to spread easily, beat in additional milk, a small amount at a time, until the desired consistency is achieved.

Canned Frostings

Commercially prepared canned frostings can also be used for cake decorating. Color it and use it for piping just like buttercream frosting. For best results, refrigerate the frosting first and keep chilled while decorating. One 16-ounce can of frosting equals about 1½ cups.

Base Frosting

Frosting cakes with a base coat is a professional technique that is simple to do, gives cakes a smoother, cleaner finish and makes frosting cakes much easier. You'll need a little more frosting than the recipe calls for, and it should be thinned slightly with a few drops of milk. Simply spread this thinned frosting on all sides of the cake after cutting and positioning all the pieces. This base coat helps to seal in the crumbs, preventing them from showing up in the final layer of frosting. Let the base coat dry for 15 to 20 minutes before covering the cake with the final layer of frosting.

Coloring Frosting

We recommend you use paste colors (available at stores carrying cake decorating supplies) because they do not thin the frosting. If liquid food coloring is used, you may need to add more powdered sugar to get the frosting back to the desired consistency.

To tint frosting with paste colors, add a small amount of the paste color with a wooden skewer and stir well. Slowly add more color until the frosting is the desired shade. With liquid food colors, add the coloring drop by drop, mixing well after each drop, until the desired shade is reached. Paste colors are available in a wide variety of colors, but you can also make almost any color by mixing the basics: red, green, yellow, blue and black.

The following chart shows how these basic colors can be mixed to produce many different frosting colors. The numbers refer to the ratio of one color to another (i.e. orange is made by mixing 1 part red food coloring with 3 parts yellow food coloring). These ratios can be used for both paste and liquid food colorings.

To make:	Red	Green	Yellow	Blue		Black
Rose	5			1	OR	1
Orange	1		3			
Peach	1		2			
Olive Green		2	1			1
Medium Blue				1		1
Purple	1			1		
Brown	2	2	1			

Storing Frosting

Buttercream frosting can be made ahead of time. Refrigerate it in an airtight container and use within two days. When ready to use it, bring the frosting to room temperature and beat well with an electric mixer.

Decorating Techniques

Frosting Cakes

To frost a cake, place a mound of frosting in the center of the cake. Spread frosting across the top by pushing it out toward the sides with a spatula—use a flexible spatula and light back-and-forth strokes. Always keep the spatula on a frosted surface, because once it touches the cake surface, crumbs will mix in with the frosting. Avoid lifting up the spatula so you don't pull the crust away from the cake. To frost the sides, work from the top down, making sure the spatula only touches frosting. After frosting, let the cake stand for at least 1 hour before slicing.

Using a Pastry Bag

A coupler can save time and mess, but it is not necessary for successful cake decorating. It is used to attach tips to the pastry bag and allows you to change tips without removing the frosting from the bag. To use, unscrew the ring, insert the cone-shaped piece into the narrow end of the pastry bag until the end extends slightly beyond the end of the bag (snip off the end of the pastry bag if necessary), then place the decorating tip on the end. Screw the ring on to hold the tip in place. To change tips, unscrew the ring, remove the tip, place the new tip on and screw the ring back in place.

To fill a pastry bag with frosting, insert the decorative tip or attach the tip with a coupler. Fold the top of the bag down as shown, then use a spatula to place frosting in the bag. Fill the bag only about half full, then unfold the top of the bag. Twist the top of the bag down tightly against the frosting.

Piped Decorations

Different decorating tips produce different piped decorations. Writing tips have round holes (in many sizes) and make smooth lines perfect for lettering and outlining. A star tip makes individual stars or fancy ridged stripes and zigzags.

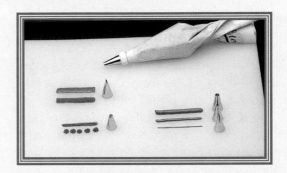

Grip the pastry bag near the top with the twisted end between your thumb and forefinger. Place the other hand near the tip as shown. Using even pressure, squeeze the frosting out while guiding the tip. Do not loosen your grip on the twisted end or the frosting will begin to push up and out at the top of the bag.

Have Fun!

Don't let yourself be limited by the colors or decorations in these photos—feel free to add your child's favorite candies to the cake, or match the frosting color to your plates or party favors. Use the recipes for inspiration and the photographs as a guide. Then let your imagination run wild!

around the World

5½ cups cake batter, divided
1 (15×15-inch) cake board, covered
1 can (16 ounces) white frosting
1 pretzel rod, broken in half
3 chocolate licorice twists
  Green gumdrops

1. Preheat oven to 350°F. Grease and flour 9-inch round cake pan, 6-ounce custard cup and medium muffin pan. Pour 3½ cups cake batter into cake pan, ½ cup cake batter into custard cup and remaining cake batter into muffin pan (¼ cup batter per muffin cup). Bake cake in pan 35 to 45 minutes, cake in custard cup about 25 minutes and cupcakes about 20 minutes or until toothpick inserted into centers comes out clean. Cool 15 minutes in pans. Loosen edges; invert onto wire racks and cool completely.

2. Trim top and side of round cake. Cut custard cup cake vertically in half. Arrange round cake, one cupcake (upside down) and half of custard cup cake on prepared cake board as shown in photo. (Reserve remaining cupcakes for another use.)

3. Reserve ½ cup frosting. Tint remaining frosting blue. Divide reserved frosting in half; tint ¼ cup frosting orange and ¼ cup green.

4. Frost entire round cake with blue frosting. Frost cupcake with green frosting and custard cup cake half with orange frosting.

5. Position pretzel rod halves to look as if they are running through globe at North and South Poles. Arrange licorice twists to connect pretzel rods to base of globe as shown in photo

6. Flatten gumdrops with rolling pin on smooth, flat surface or sheet of waxed paper sprinkled with sugar. Roll until very thin (about ¹⁄₁₆ inch), turning frequently to coat with sugar. Cut gumdrops into shapes of continents with sharp knife or scissors. Arrange continents on globe as shown in photo.

Makes 12 to 14 servings

cake tip
If your cake turns out relatively flat on top, you might not need to trim it. Simply turn the cake over and frost the flatter base of the cake.

batter up

5½ cups cake batter, divided
1 (15×15-inch) cake board, covered, or large plate
1 can (16 ounces) white frosting
1 miniature chocolate sandwich cookie

1. Preheat oven to 350°F. Grease and flour 2-quart ovenproof bowl and 8-inch round cake pan. Pour 3½ cups cake batter into prepared bowl; pour 2 cups cake batter into cake pan. Bake cake in bowl 55 to 60 minutes and cake in pan 20 to 30 minutes or until wooden skewer inserted into centers comes out clean. Cool 15 minutes in pans. Loosen edges; invert onto wire racks and cool completely.

2. Trim flat side of bowl cake and top of round cake. Cut round cake into crescent shape to create rim of hat as shown in photo. Place rim piece on prepared cake board. Place bowl cake next to rim cake to form baseball hat.

3. Tint ⅓ cup frosting blue. Tint remaining frosting orange.

4. Frost rim and bowl of cap with orange frosting. Place blue frosting in small plastic food storage bag. Cut tip off one corner of bag and pipe blue lines on cap as shown in photo. Open sandwich cookie; place half of cookie, filling side down, on top of hat.

Makes 14 to 18 servings

cake tip

This cake is a baseball fan's dream come true! Decorate the cap with the colors of your child's favorite team or one that he or she plays on. Party supply stores carry invitations that look like tickets to sporting events, and baseball cards or team t-shirts make great party favors in keeping with the theme. Best of all, there's no question what you should feed the kids before the cake: hot dogs, perhaps with peanuts and soft pretzels on the side.

burger Mania

9½ cups cake batter, divided
1 (10-inch) round cake board,
covered, or large plate
1 can (16 ounces) white frosting
1 can (16 ounces) chocolate
frosting
12 green gumdrops
1 to 2 tablespoons sunflower seeds

1. Preheat oven to 350°F. Grease and flour 2-quart ovenproof bowl and 2 (8-inch) round cake pans. Pour 4 cups cake batter into prepared bowl; pour 2¾ cups cake batter into each cake pan. Bake cake in bowl 60 to 70 minutes and cakes in pans about 35 minutes or until wooden skewer inserted into centers comes out clean. Cool 15 minutes in pans. Loosen edges; invert onto wire racks and cool completely.

2. Trim flat side of bowl cake and tops of round cakes.

3. Reserve ½ cup white frosting; set aside. Blend ¼ cup chocolate frosting with remaining white frosting to create tan color.

4. Place one round cake layer on prepared cake board. Frost with tan frosting. Top with second round cake layer; frost with chocolate frosting. Place bowl cake, flat side down, on top of chocolate frosted layer; frost with tan frosting.

5. Flatten gumdrops with rolling pin on smooth, flat surface or sheet of waxed paper sprinkled with sugar. Roll until very thin (about ¹⁄₁₆ inch), turning frequently to coat with sugar. Cut ruffled edge on

gumdrops with sharp knife or scissors; tuck underneath chocolate frosted layer to resemble pickles.

6. Divide reserved white frosting in half; tint half red and half yellow. Using medium writing tip, pipe frosting around edges of bowl cake to resemble ketchup and mustard. Sprinkle sunflower seeds on top of cake.

Makes 34 to 38 servings

cake tip
This burger cake is always a kid-pleaser, but adults will love it too! It's perfect for many other occasions besides birthdays—serve it up at a Memorial Day, Fourth of July or Labor Day barbecue, or any casual get-together.

buzzz

4 cups cake batter
1 (10-inch) round cake board, covered, or large plate
1¾ cups prepared white frosting or Buttercream Frosting (page 92)
Assorted black, yellow and red candies
Black licorice twists

1. Preheat oven to 350°F. Grease and flour 2½-quart ovenproof bowl. Pour cake batter into prepared bowl. Bake 60 to 70 minutes or until wooden skewer inserted into center comes out clean. Cool 15 minutes in bowl. Loosen edge; invert onto wire rack and cool completely.

2. Trim flat side of cake. Turn cake over and cut small piece from top of cake to slightly flatten back of bee, if desired. Place cake on prepared cake board.

3. Reserve ¼ cup white frosting. Tint ¾ cup frosting black and ¾ cup frosting yellow.

4. Using wooden toothpick, mark semicircle about 3½ inches from one edge of cake for face, and three parallel semicircles for rest of body.

5. Frost face with reserved white frosting. Alternately frost body sections with yellow and black, piping frosting with floral tip to create fuzzy texture, if desired. Reserve small portion of black frosting for piping.

6. Using medium writing tip and reserved black frosting, pipe line between head and body.

7. Arrange assorted candies and licorice twists for face, antennae, legs, wings and stinger as shown in photo.
Makes 14 to 18 servings

cake tip
Bowl cakes, like bundt cakes and pound cakes, should be tested for doneness with a wooden skewer (since toothpicks are not long enough to do the job). Wooden skewers are commonly sold in supermakets, but if you can't find them, a dry (uncooked) piece of spaghetti may be used as a substitute.

Campfire fun

2 (9-inch) square chocolate cake
  layers
1 (10-inch) square cake board,
  covered, or large plate
1 cup chocolate chips
½ cup heavy cream
2¼ cups prepared white frosting,
  divided
¾ cup marshmallow creme
1 tablespoon unsweetened cocoa
  powder
¼ cup graham cracker crumbs
¼ cup peanut butter chips

1. Trim tops and sides of cake layers. Place one layer on prepared cake board.

2. For chocolate filling, heat chocolate chips and cream in microwavable bowl at HIGH 1 minute or until chocolate is melted; stir until smooth. Chill 10 minutes, stirring occasionally, or until filling reaches desired consistency. (Filling will thicken as it cools.)

3. For marshmallow filling, combine ¾ cup frosting and marshmallow creme in small bowl; stir until smooth.

4. Combine remaining 1½ cups frosting and cocoa; stir until smooth. Frost sides of bottom cake layer with cocoa frosting; let stand 10 minutes to set frosting.

5. Spread chocolate filling over cake layer, allowing some filling to run over edges. Spread marshmallow filling over chocolate filling, allowing some filling to run over edges. Place second cake layer over marshmallow filling.

6. Frost top and sides of top cake layer with cocoa frosting. Sprinkle graham cracker crumbs over top of cake; press in lightly. Arrrange peanut butter chips over top of cake. Score cake down center to resemble graham cracker perforations as shown in photo.

Makes 16 to 18 servings

cake tips •••••••••••••••••••

When baking layer cakes such as this one, it's important to divide the cake batter equally between the pans to make even layers. Either measure the batter and divide it equally (for example, 2 cups of batter in each pan) or weigh the pans after adding the batter. Spread the batter evenly in the pans and tap the pans on the countertop to remove air bubbles before baking.

If you're using a cake mix, you can estimate that one standard size package (about 18 ounces) yields approximately 5½ cups batter, so a 2-layer cake should get 2¾ cups batter in each pan.

Carousel Cake

1 (10-inch) bundt cake
1 (10-inch) round cake board,
   covered, or large plate
1 can (16 ounces) white frosting
   Assorted animal-shaped cookies
   Decorator gel (optional)
   Assorted candies and decors
   Colored or striped drinking
      straws
   Paper carousel roof (see Cake
      Tip)

1. Place cake on prepared cake board.

2. Tint frosting orange.

3. Frost cake with orange frosting, allowing frosting to drip down side of cake.

4. Outline animal-shaped cookies with decorator gel, if desired; arrange cookies on top of cake. Press candies and decors lightly into frosting.

5. Place straws around cake to support carousel roof; carefully set roof on top of straws.   *Makes 14 to 16 servings*

cake tip••••••••••••••••••••••••••••
     To create carousel roof, cut out a 7½-inch circle from 8½×11-inch sheet of colored construction paper. Cut one slit from outer edge of circle to center; tape cut edges together to form carousel roof. If a two-color roof is desired, cut a second 7½-inch circle from construction paper in another color and fold into eight wedges. Carefully cut out four wedges; glue them onto first circle of paper so colors alternate (before cutting the slit and taping the edges).

Catch Some Rays

1 (9-inch) round cake
1 (15×15-inch) cake board,
   covered, or large platter
1 can (16 ounces) white frosting
6 sugar ice cream cones
   Red fruit rollups
   Red licorice whip

1. Trim top and side of cake; place on prepared cake board.

2. Tint frosting yellow.

3. Frost cake and ice cream cones with yellow frosting.

4. Cut two small slits about 1 inch apart in side of cake with small knife. (Slits should be parallel to top of cake.) Slide wide end of one cone into slits, securing cone to cake. Repeat with remaining cones to create sun's rays.

5. Cut sunglass shapes from fruit rollups and place on cake. Add licorice pieces to create sunglasses and smile.

Makes 10 to 12 servings

cake tips ●●●●●●●●●●●●●●●●●●●

To get bright colors—like the one used for this sun—and keep the frosting the proper consistency, tint the frosting with paste food colorings. Add a small amount of the paste color with a wooden skewer or toothpick, then stir well. Slowly add more color until the frosting is the desired shade.

To frost a single layer cake, spoon a mound of frosting in the center and spread it outward to all edges. Be careful not to mix crumbs into the frosting. Before decorating the cake, carefully smooth the frosting. Hold a narrow metal spatula under hot running water, shake off the excess water and use the damp spatula to quickly smooth a section of frosting with long strokes in one direction. Repeat dampening and smoothing until the frosting is smooth on the cake top and sides.

catch some rays

Crayon Craze

1 (13×9-inch) cake
1 (14×10-inch) cake board,
    covered, or large platter
2 cans (16 ounces each) white
    frosting
4 flat-bottomed ice cream cones

1. Trim top and sides of cake. Measure 4½ inches down long sides of cake; draw line across top of cake with wooden toothpick to create 9×4½-inch rectangle. Using toothpick line as guide, carefully cut halfway through cake (about 1 inch). Do *not* cut all the way through cake.

2. Cut cake in half horizontally from 9-inch side just to horizontal cut made at 4½-inch line. Remove 9×4½×1-inch piece of cake; reserve for another use. Round edges of 9-inch side to resemble top of crayon box as shown in photo. Place cake on prepared cake board.

3. Tint one can frosting gold. Tint 1 cup frosting green. Divide remaining frosting into four parts, (about ¼ cup each). Tint one part red, one yellow, one orange and one blue.

4. Frost entire cake with gold frosting. Using medium writing tip and green frosting, pipe the word CRAYONS on cake. Pipe stripes and two green triangles on bottom of box and decorative borders around box as shown in photo.

5. Gently cut ice cream cones in half vertically with serrated knife. Frost each cone different color (red, yellow, orange and blue). Place frosted cones on cake, just below rounded edge to resemble crayon tips.

Makes 16 to 18 servings

cake tips

Since many decorated cakes are too large for standard plates, cake boards (available at any stores that carry cake decorating supplies) are always a good option. But you may already have something on hand that will work just as well. You can use platters, cutting boards, cookie sheets or any other large flat surfaces.

Remember to tuck strips of waxed paper underneath the cake before frosting it so your platter or cake board stays clean. When the decorating is complete, carefully slide out the strips and touch up the frosting as needed.

dream Castle

3 (8-inch) square cake layers
1 (19×13-inch) cake board, cut in half crosswise and covered
5¼ cups prepared white frosting or Buttercream Frosting (page 92)
Assorted colored sugar
4 sugar ice cream cones
Small purple and white gumdrops
Pastel candy-coated chocolate pieces
2 pink sugar wafer cookies

Diagrams 1 & 2

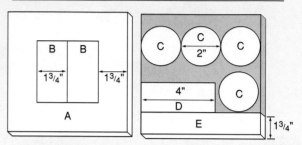

Diagram 3

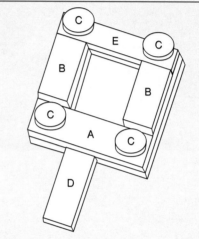

1. Trim top and sides of cake layers. Place one layer on prepared cake board. Tint ½ cup frosting blue and ½ cup yellow. Frost top of cake layer with some of remaining 4¼ cups white frosting.

2. Cut remaining 2 cake layers as shown in Diagrams 1 and 2.

3. Place piece A over bottom layer. Frost top of piece A with some white frosting.

4. Position remaining pieces as shown in Diagram 3, connecting with some white frosting.

5. Frost entire cake with white frosting. Cover piece D (bridge) with colored sugar.

6. Frost 2 cones with blue frosting and 2 cones with yellow frosting. Place as shown in photo.

7. Decorate castle and towers as shown, using frosting to attach gumdrops and chocolate pieces, if needed. Arrange wafer cookies on front of castle for gate.
Makes 14 to 16 servings

party tips ●●●●●●●●●●●●●●●●●●

If your child wants a Dream Castle cake, chances are good that he or she will like a party with a royal theme. Create party invitations with a royal flair and seal them with gold foil seals. Turn a dining room chair into a throne for your guest of honor—decorate it with crepe paper, ribbon and lots of balloons. Purchase crowns at a party-supply store and let the kids decorate them with sequins, beads and glitter. For party favors, consider small storybooks, fairy tale coloring books and gold foil-wrapped chocolate coins.

dream castle

flower Power

1 (9-inch) round cake
1 (10-inch) round cake board,
    covered, or large plate
1¼ cups prepared white frosting or
    Buttercream Frosting (page 92)
7 rectangular gummy candies
Assorted candies
15 to 20 round green candies
1 chocolate licorice twist

1. Cut cake into flower shape as shown in photo. Place on prepared cake board.

2. Reserve ¼ cup frosting. Tint remaining 1 cup frosting pink.

3. Frost entire cake with pink frosting; pipe decorative edge around cake, if desired. Pipe or spread circle of reserved white frosting in center of cake.

4. Flatten gummy candies with rolling pin on smooth, flat surface or sheet of waxed paper sprinkled with sugar. Roll until ⅛ to ¼ inch thick, turning frequently to coat with sugar. Cut out petal shapes with sharp knife or scissors. Arrange petals on cake; decorate flower face with assorted candies.

5. Thread round green candies through licorice twist to resemble stem, reserving several candies for leaves. Insert end of stem into cake; arrange candy "leaves" around stem as shown in photo.

Makes 10 to 12 servings

cake tip

It's best to bake the cake the day before you plan to cut and decorate it if possible. A freshly baked cake can be difficult to work with as it may be too tender. If you don't have time to bake the cake the day ahead, place the cooled cake in the freezer for 30 to 45 minutes before cutting and decorating. Freezing the cake before cutting allows you to get the cleanest edges with the least amount of crumbs.

flutter away

2 (9-inch) round cake layers
2 individual chocolate-covered
cake rolls
1 (15×15-inch) cake board,
covered, or large platter
1 can (16 ounces) white frosting
20 miniature chocolate sandwich
cookies
1 chocolate sandwich cookie
2 chocolate licorice twists
2 candy-coated chocolate pieces

Diagram

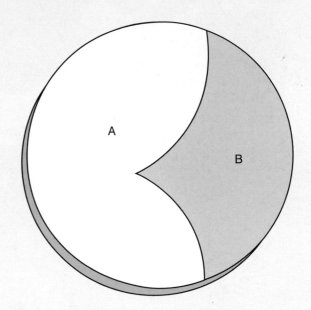

1. Trim top and sides of cake layers. Using diagram as guide, draw pattern for butterfly wing (piece A) on 9-inch circle of waxed paper. Cut pattern out and place on one cake layer. Cut out wing; reserve piece B for another use. Repeat with second cake layer.

2. Place cake rolls end to end in center of prepared cake board. Arrange wing pieces on either side of cake rolls to form butterfly shape.

3. Tint frosting orange.

4. Frost wings with orange frosting. Arrange 7 miniature sandwich cookies on each set of wings.

5. Place 4 miniature sandwich cookies on top of chocolate cake rolls to form butterfly's body. Attach regular size sandwich cookie for head and licorice twists for anntenae. Open remaining 2 miniature sandwich cookies to expose white filling; place opened cookies under antennae for eyes. Arrange candies over white filling as shown in photo.

Makes 16 to 20 servings

fun & games

1 (13×9-inch) cake
1 (19×13-inch) cake board, cut in
    half crosswise and covered
2 cans (16 ounces each) white
    frosting
    Black licorice twists
3 miniature chocolate sandwich
    cookies

1. Trim top and sides of cake. Trim two corners of 9-inch side of cake, rounding edges slightly as shown in photo.

2. Tint 1¾ cans frosting green. Tint remining frosting gray.

3. Frost entire cake with green frosting. Frost rectangular box on top of green frosting with gray frosting to resemble screen. Use wooden skewer or paring knife to score gray frosting as shown in photo.

4. Arrange licorice twists around screen. Decorate computer game with sandwich cookies and pieces of licorice twists to resembe control buttons and speaker as shown in photo.

Makes 16 to 20 servings

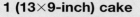 cake tip••••••••••••••••••••••••
    The consistency of your frosting is an important factor in cake decorating. Commercially prepared canned frosting works well, but you may encounter a few of the same problems that arise with homemade frosting. If the frosting is too soft because your kitchen is warm, refrigerate the frosting for about 15 minutes and keep it chilled while you work. If the frosting is too thin because of liquid food coloring that was added, beat in some sifted powdered sugar.

go fish

1 (9-inch) round cake
1 (14×10-inch) cake board,
covered, or large platter
1½ cups prepared white frosting or
Buttercream Frosting (page 92)
Assorted hard and gummy
candies
Red pull-apart licorice twists

1. Trim top and side of cake. Using Diagram 1 as guide, draw fish pattern on 9-inch circle of waxed paper. Cut pattern out and place on cake. Cut as shown in Diagram 1.

2. Position pieces A and B on prepared cake board as shown in Diagram 2, connecting with small amount of frosting.

3. Tint ⅓ of frosting green, ⅓ orange and ⅓ yellow.

4. Frost front third of fish green, middle third orange and back third yellow.

5. Arrange candies in rows on middle third of fish; position candies for eye and mouth as shown in photo.

6. Cut licorice into 2- to 3-inch lengths; arrange on cake to form top and bottom fins as shown in photo. (Trim licorice pieces to fit as needed.)

7. Cut additional licorice into longer pieces to decorate tail as shown in photo, trimming licorice as needed.

Makes 10 to 12 servings

Diagram 1

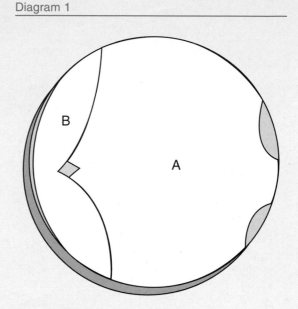

Diagram 2

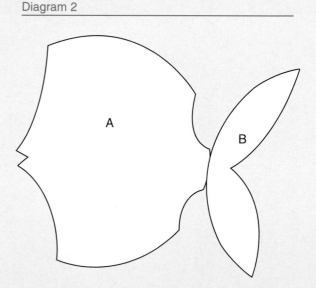

hocus Pocus

1 (13×9-inch) cake
1 (19×13-inch) cake board, cut in half crosswise and covered, or large platter
1½ cups prepared white frosting or Buttercream Frosting (page 92)
Yellow rectangular gummy candies

1. Trim top and sides of cake. Using diagram as guide, draw hat pattern on 13×9-inch piece of waxed paper. Cut pattern out and place on cake. Cut out hat; place on prepared cake board.

2. Tint frosting blue.

3. Frost entire cake with blue frosting.

4. Flatten gummy candies with rolling pin on smooth, flat surface or sheet of waxed paper sprinkled with sugar. Roll until very thin (about ¹⁄₁₆ inch), turning frequently to coat with sugar. Cut out star and crescent shapes with sharp knife or scissors.

5. Arrange stars and crescents on cake as shown in photo.

Makes 12 to 16 servings

Diagram

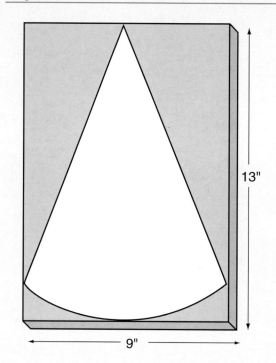

13"

9"

island fun

1 (13×9-inch) cake
1 (14×10-inch) cake board, covered
1 can (16 ounces) white frosting
1½ cups graham cracker crumbs
6 green gumdrops
1 pretzel rod, broken in half
   Small bear-shaped graham
     cookies
   Assorted decorator gels (optional)
   Assorted candies and goldfish
     crackers

1. Trim top and sides of cake. Place on prepared cake board.

2. Tint frosting blue.

3. Frost entire cake with blue frosting. Spoon graham cracker crumbs onto frosting to resemble desert island.

4. Flatten gumdrops with rolling pin on smooth, flat surface or sheet of waxed paper sprinkled with sugar. Roll until very thin (about ¹⁄₁₆ inch), turning frequently to coat with sugar. Cut each gumdrop into leaf shape with sharp knife or scissors. Position pretzel rod half near center of island; carefully attach leaves to top of pretzel to form palm tree as shown in photo.

5. Decorate bear-shaped cookies with decorator gels, if desired. Arrange bear-shaped cookies, candies and goldfish crackers on cake as shown in photo.

Makes 16 to 20 servings

cake tip •••••••••••••••••••
   Let your imagination—and the kids'—run wild with this cake. Kids can decorate goldfish crackers and bear-shaped cookies as shown in the photo, or they can fill the waters around the island with gummy fish, sharks and other aquatic creatures.

it's my Party

5½ cups cake batter, divided
1 (10-inch) round cake board,
covered, or large plate
2 cans (16 ounces each) white
frosting
1 doll
Assorted candies and decors

1. Preheat oven to 350°F. Grease and flour 2-quart ovenproof bowl and 8-inch round cake pan. Pour 3½ cups cake batter into prepared bowl; pour 2 cups cake batter into cake pan. Bake cake in bowl 55 to 60 minutes and cake in pan 25 to 30 minutes or until wooden skewer inserted into centers comes out clean. Cool 15 minutes in pans. Loosen edges; invert onto wire racks and cool completely.

2. Trim flat side of bowl cake. Trim side of round cake so edge is even with bowl cake. Place round cake on prepared cake board.

3. Frost top of round cake lightly with frosting. Place bowl cake, flat side down, on top of round cake.

4. Tint 1 cup frosting purple.

5. Frost entire cake with white frosting.

6. Make small cut in center of cake and insert doll into cake. (To keep doll's clothing clean, wrap bottom of doll in plastic wrap.)

7. Using medium writing tip and purple frosting, pipe designs on party dress. Decorate with assorted candies and decors as shown in photo.

Makes 14 to 18 servings

cake tip ●●●●●●●●●●●●●●●●●●●●●● This cake makes a great centerpiece for a birthday party, especially when your guest of honor chooses the colors and decors for the cake. To make it truly unique, decorate the cake to match one of your daughter's favorite dresses (or, if she prefers, one of her doll's dresses).

let it Snow

2 (9-inch) round cake layers
2 (10-inch) round cake boards,
   taped together and covered, or
   large tray
1½ cups prepared white frosting or
   Buttercream Frosting (page 92)
½ cup prepared chocolate frosting
   or Chocolate Buttercream
   Frosting (page 93)
   Assorted gumdrops
1 sugar ice cream cone, cut in half
   crosswise
   Red pull-apart licorice twists

Diagram

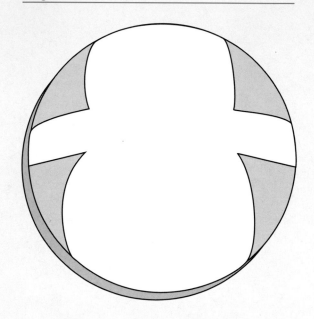

1. Trim tops and sides of cake layers. Cut off small piece from one side of each cake to form flat edge (so cake layers will fit together as shown in photo).

2. Using diagram as guide, draw pattern for snowman's head (with hat) on 9-inch circle of waxed paper. Cut pattern out and place on top half of cake. Cut out head. Place top and bottom parts of snowman on prepared cake board; attach flat edges of cake layers with small amount of white frosting.

3. Frost hat with chocolate frosting. Frost remaining cake with white frosting.

4. Decorate snowman with assorted gumdrops and ice cream cone nose as shown in photo. Arrange licorice to resemble hatband and scarf as shown in photo.   *Makes 16 to 18 servings*

look Who's One

1 (13×9-inch) cake
1 (19×13-inch) cake board, cut in
half crosswise and covered
1½ cups prepared white frosting or
Buttercream Frosting (page 92)
Assorted colored candies

1. Trim top and sides of cake. Using diagram as guide, draw number 1 pattern on 13×9-inch piece of waxed paper. Cut pattern out and place on cake. Cut out number 1; place on prepared cake board.

2. Tint frosting yellow.

3. Frost cake with yellow frosting.

4. Decorate with assorted candies as shown in photo.

Makes 12 to 16 servings

 cake tip

Try using a novelty cake mix instead of a plain one for a change of pace. Mixes that add swirls or confetti to the batter provide an unexpected bit of color when you cut into the cake.

Diagram

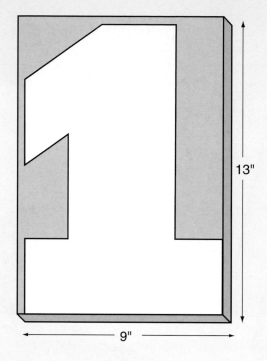

13"

9"

mr. moon

1 (9-inch) round cake
1 (10-inch) round cake board,
    covered, or large plate
1 can (16 ounces) white frosting
    Red licorice whip

Diagram

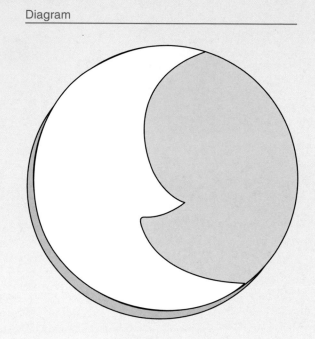

1. Trim top of cake. Using diagram as guide, draw moon pattern on 9-inch circle of waxed paper. Cut pattern out and place on cake. Cut out moon; reserve remaining cake for another use. Place moon on prepared cake board.

2. Tint frosting yellow.

3. Frost entire cake with yellow frosting.

4. Create moon face with pieces of licorice as shown in photo.

Makes 6 to 8 servings

cake tips ••••••••••••••••••••••
Once the frosting is on the cake, use a flexible metal pastry spatula to create decorative swirls and other finishing touches. For creamy or butter-based frostings, dip the spatula in cold water every so often so the frosting will stay on the cake and not stick to the spatula.

For cakes like this one where a sizable portion of the cake is cut out, you may want to serve the cut-out pieces as well. Cut these remaining cake pieces into squares or chunks, frost them (with the same color or choose a complementary one) and decorate them with a few candies or assorted decors.

nessie

2 (10-inch) bundt cakes
2½ cups prepared white frosting or
    Buttercream Frosting (page 92)
1 (40×20-inch) cake board, covered
    Gumballs, assorted candies and
    red licorice twist

1. Cut one bundt cake in half. Cut second bundt cake in quarters; set aside two quarters for another use.

2. Tint frosting light purple.

3. Frost two bundt cake halves with frosting, covering all sides of cake except two cut surfaces on each half. Frost two bundt cake quarters with frosting, covering all sides of cake except one cut surface on each quarter.

4. Stand two bundt cake halves on their cut surfaces, positioning them end to end in center of prepared cake board. Place bundt cake quarters, unfrosted cut surfaces down, on either side of bundt cake halves to resemble Loch Ness monster's head and tail as shown in photo.

5. Decorate monster with gumballs, assorted candies and licorice as shown in photo.

Makes 24 to 28 servings

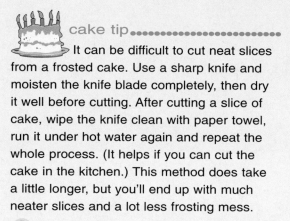

cake tip

It can be difficult to cut neat slices from a frosted cake. Use a sharp knife and moisten the knife blade completely, then dry it well before cutting. After cutting a slice of cake, wipe the knife clean with paper towel, run it under hot water again and repeat the whole process. (It helps if you can cut the cake in the kitchen.) This method does take a little longer, but you'll end up with much neater slices and a lot less frosting mess.

On the go

1 (13×9-inch) cake

1 (19×13-inch) cake board, cut in half crosswise and covered

2½ cups prepared white frosting or Buttercream Frosting (page 92)

12 chocolate and vanilla sandwich cookies

Assorted candies and red licorice whips

1. Using diagram as guide, draw skate pattern on 13×9-inch piece of waxed paper. Cut pattern out and place on cake. Cut out pieces as shown in Diagram 1.

2. Position pieces A, B and C on prepared cake board as shown in Diagram 2, connecting pieces with small amount of frosting. Discard piece D.

3. Tint frosting light blue.

4. Frost entire cake with blue frosting.

5. Stack 3 cookies for each wheel, attaching with frosting. Decorate skate with candies and licorice as shown in photo. *Makes 12 to 16 servings*

Diagram 1

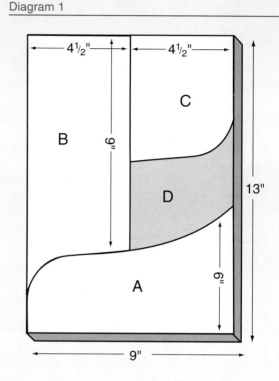

Diagram 2

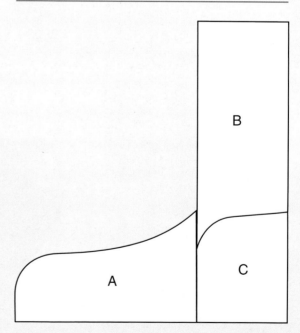

One Scoop or two?

5½ cups cake batter, divided
1 (14×10-inch) prepared cake board, covered, or large plate
1 can (16 ounces) chocolate fudge frosting
1 can (16 ounces) white frosting
Red licorice whip

1. Preheat oven to 350°F. Grease and flour 9-inch round cake pan and medium muffin pan. Pour 3½ cups cake batter into cake pan; pour remaining cake batter into muffin pan (¼ cup batter per muffin cup). Bake cake in pan 35 to 45 minutes and cupcakes about 20 minutes or until toothpick inserted into centers comes out clean. Cool 15 minutes in pans. Loosen edges; invert onto wire racks and cool completely.

2. Trim top of cake and one cupcake. (Reserve remaining cupcakes for another use.) Using Diagram 1 as guide, draw bowl pattern on 9-inch circle of waxed paper. Cut pattern out and place on cake. Cut out pieces from cake. Place cake on prepared cake board, using larger half of piece A as bowl and smaller half as scoop of ice cream. Invert piece B; place beneath bottom half of cake (bowl) to resemble foot of bowl as shown in Diagram 2. Discard piece C. Place cupcake on top of ice cream scoop for cherry.

3. Reserve 1 cup chocolate frosting; frost bottom half of cake (bowl) with remaining chocolate frosting. Draw lines in bowl with toothpick or knife as shown in photo. Reserve ½ cup white frosting; frost top half of cake (ice cream) with remaining white frosting.

4. Thin reserved chocolate frosting slightly with water. Fill plastic food storage bag with thinned chocolate frosting; cut off tip of bag in one corner and use to pipe "chocolate sauce" on top of ice cream scoop. (Thinned frosting will appear more like hot fudge.)

5. Tint reserved white frosting red; frost cupcake with red frosting. Top with piece of licorice to resemble cherry stem.

Makes 10 to 12 servings

Diagram 1

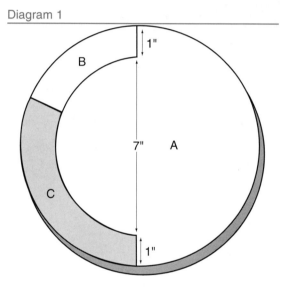

Diagram 2

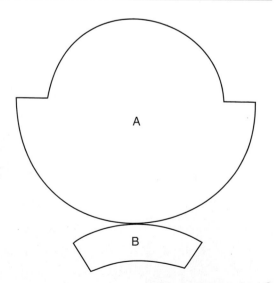

one scoop or two?

Out of this World

4½ cups cake batter, divided
1 (10-inch) round cake board, covered, or large plate
2 cups prepared white frosting or Buttercream Frosting (page 92)
Red decorator gel
Black licorice twists
8 to 10 large gumballs
Assorted candies

1. Preheat oven to 350°F. Grease and flour 9-inch round cake pan and 1½-quart ovenproof bowl. Pour 2¾ cups cake batter into cake pan; pour 1¾ cups cake batter into prepared bowl. Bake cake in pan 30 to 35 minutes and cake in bowl 45 to 55 minutes or until wooden skewer inserted into centers comes out clean. Cool 15 minutes in pans. Loosen edges; invert onto wire racks and cool completely.

2. Trim top of bowl cake and top and side of round cake. Place round cake on prepared cake board. Spread small amount of frosting on center of round cake. Place bowl cake, flat side down, on top of round cake.

3. Reserve ½ cup frosting. Tint remaining 1½ cups frosting blue-gray.

4. Frost entire cake with blue-gray frosting. Frost top half of round cake with reserved white frosting (over blue-gray frosting). Cover top of round cake with red decorator gel.

5. Cut licorice into 1½-inch pieces; arrange around side of bowl cake over white frosting as shown in photo. Decorate UFO with gumballs and assorted candies as shown in photo.

Makes 12 to 14 servings

cake tip ●●●●●●●●●●●●●●●●●●●●●●●●●●
When baking bowl-shaped cakes, it's important to be certain that the bowls you use are ovenproof. Ovenproof glassware, such as Pyrex, is available at many supermarkets and in stores that carry housewares. If you don't know the size of your bowl, simply measure how many cups of water it holds—that is the bowl size.

Party time

5½ cups cake batter, divided
1 (14-inch round) cake board,
    covered, or large plate
1½ cups prepared white frosting or
    Buttercream Frosting (page 92)
    Black and green decorator gels
    Black licorice twists
    Red licorice rope
    Assorted candies
2 gum-filled lollipops

1. Preheat oven to 350°F. Grease and flour 9-inch round cake pan and medium muffin pan. Pour 3½ cups cake batter into cake pan; pour remaining cake batter into muffin pan (¼ cup batter per muffin cup). Bake cake in pan 35 to 45 minutes and cupcakes 18 to 20 minutes or until toothpick inserted into centers comes out clean. Cool 15 minutes in pans. Loosen edges; invert onto wire racks and cool completely.

2. Trim top and side of round cake and two cupcakes. (Reserve remaining cupcakes for another use.) Place round cake on prepared cake board.

3. Tint half of frosting purple.

4. Frost top of round cake with white frosting. Frost side of cake and cupcakes with purple frosting. Position cupcakes with tops against side of round cake as shown in photo; attach cupcakes to cake with small amount of purple frosting. Pipe decorative edge around face of clock and edge of cupcakes, if desired.

5. Pipe numbers and dots on face of clock with decorator gels. Arrange licorice and candies for clock hands and stopper as shown in photo.

6. Insert lollipops into bottom of clock for feet.   *Makes 12 to 14 servings*

cake tip
Even if you're using a cake mix, it's still important to have good, sturdy pans for baking. A cake pan, or layer pan, is round with a straight side at least 1½ inches high. Choose aluminum or heavy-gauge steel to produce a cake with a delicate, tender crust. Besides the most common round 8- or 9-inch cake pans, there is a wide array of pans available that measure from 3 to 24 inches in diameter. Cake pans also come in a variety of specialty shapes.

Peanut

2 (8-inch) round cake layers
1 (14×10-inch) cake board,
    covered, or large platter
2 cans (16 ounces each) white
    frosting
1 flat-bottomed ice cream cone
2 gumdrops
    Red licorice whip

1. Trim tops and sides of cake layers. Cut one cake layer in half.

2. Place round cake on prepared cake board. Place cake halves on either side of round cake to form ears as shown in photo.

3. Tint frosting pink.

4. Frost entire cake with pink frosting. Cut off top of ice cream cone with serrated knife. Frost cone with pink frosting; place on round cake to form trunk.

5. Decorate elephant with gumdrops and pieces of licorice as shown in photo.
Makes 14 to 16 servings

cake tips
When baking two cake layers, place them both on one rack positioned in the center of the oven. Make sure there is enough space between them so air can circulate freely and the layers will cook evenly. Rotate the pans (front to back or side to side) halfway through the cooking time.

In addition to testing cakes for doneness with a toothpick (where a clean toothpick indicates that a cake is done), there are other ways to check if a cake is done. First, look at the color—a baked yellow cake should be golden brown, white cake should be light brown and chocolate cake should deepen in color. Next, look at the sides of the pan—a cake that's done will be just starting to pull away from the sides of the pan. Finally, press your fingertips lightly in the center of the cake. If the cake springs back and does not leave an indentation, the cake is done.

Picasso's Palette

1 (9-inch) round cake
1 (10-inch) round cake board,
   covered, or large plate
1 cup prepared white frosting or
   Buttercream Frosting (page 92)
   Assorted color decorator gels
   Red pull-apart licorice twist
1 pretzel rod

1. Trim top and side of cake. Cut out small circle on one side of cake; cut piece from side of cake to create palette shape as shown in photo. Place on prepared cake board.

2. Tint frosting light brown.

3. Frost entire cake with brown frosting.

4. Pipe spots of paint on palette with decorator gels.

5. Create artist's paintbrush by cutting 2-inch lengths of licorice and connecting them to pretzel rod with foil as shown in photo.   *Makes 10 to 12 servings*

cake tips ••••••••••••••••••

If you like to plan ahead, you may want to bake your cake in advance and freeze it, leaving just the decorating for the day of the party. To freeze unfrosted cakes, first be sure they have cooled completely. Then wrap them well in heavy-duty aluminum foil and place them in resealable freezer bags. Store the cakes in the coldest part of the freezer (the back or the bottom) for up to 2 months.

To thaw a frozen cake for frosting, remove it from the freezer bag and place it on the counter, opening up the foil wrapping so the cake can breathe as it thaws. (This allows the moisture to escape so the cake won't get soggy.) Let the cake thaw completely before frosting.

Prince the frog

1 (13×9-inch) cake
1 (14×10-inch) cake board,
    covered, or large platter
2 medium cupcakes
2 cans (16 ounces each) white
    frosting
2 miniature powdered sugar
    doughnuts
2 miniature chocolate sandwich
    cookies
  Assorted candies

1. Trim top and sides of cake. Using diagram as guide, draw frog pattern on 13×9-inch piece of waxed paper. Cut pattern out and place on cake. Cut out frog; place on prepared cake board. Position cupcakes next to cake to form eyes.

2. Reserve ½ cup frosting. Tint remaining frosting green.

3. Frost entire cake and cupcakes with green frosting.

4. Using medium writing tip and reserved white frosting, pipe outline of frog on cake. Place doughnuts on top of cupcakes for eyes; place sandwich cookies on top of doughnuts.

5. Add assorted candies to create frog's mouth and feet as shown in photo.

Makes 14 to 18 servings

Diagram

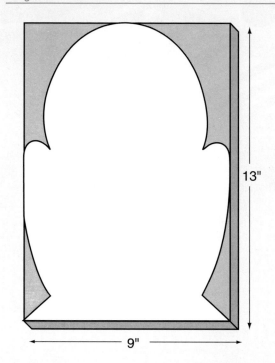

13"

9"

Puppy love

1 (13×9-inch) cake
1 (19×13-inch) cake board, cut in
    half crosswise and covered, or
    large platter
1½ cups prepared white frosting or
    Buttercream Frosting (page 92)
    Black decorator gel
    Red fruit rollup
10 to 12 miniature chocolate
    sandwich cookies
    Assorted candies

1. Trim top and sides of cake. Using diagram as guide, draw puppy pattern on 13×9-inch piece of waxed paper. Cut pattern out and place on cake. Cut out puppy; place on prepared cake board.

2. Frost entire cake with white frosting.

3. Pipe outline of puppy, nose, ears, eyes, eyebrows and mouth with black decorator gel as shown in photo.

4. Cut two pieces of fruit rollup to fit inside ears.

5. Arrange sandwich cookies over puppy to resemble spots. Create teeth, eyes and collar with candies as shown in photo.　　　*Makes 14 to 16 servings*

Diagram

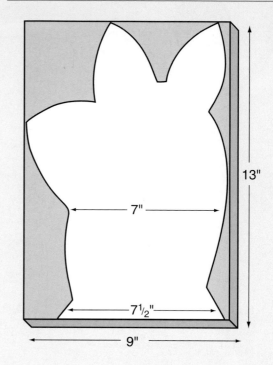

13"

7"

7½"

9"

Scared Silly

5½ cups cake batter, divided
1 (15×15-inch) cake board, covered, or large platter
1 can (16 ounces) white frosting
2 pretzel rods
2 gum-filled lollipops
2 miniature powdered sugar doughnuts
Assorted candies

1. Preheat oven to 350°F. Grease and flour 2-quart ovenproof bowl and medium muffin pan. Pour 4 cups cake batter into prepared bowl; pour remaining cake batter into muffin pan (¼ cup batter per muffin cup). Bake cake in bowl 60 to 70 minutes and cupcakes about 20 minutes or until wooden skewer inserted into centers comes out clean. Cool 15 minutes in pans. Loosen edges; invert onto wire racks and cool completely.

2. Trim flat side of bowl cake and tops of 2 cupcakes. (Reserve remaining cupcakes for another use.) Place cake on prepared cake board.

3. Tint frosting purple.

4. Frost entire cake and cupcakes with purple frosting.

5. Press pretzel rods into cake about 3 inches apart; press cupcakes into other ends of pretzel rods to create legs and feet of monster. Press lollipops into side of cake to create arms.

6. Position doughnuts on monster for eyes; add assorted candies to create tongue, teeth and toes.

Makes 14 to 18 servings

cake tip

If you want to make a mix cake extra special, try adding nuts, chocolate chips or chopped candy to the batter. Simply toss them with a little bit of the dry cake mix before stirring them in to prevent them from sinking to the bottom of the pan. (If you are adding these ingredients to a scratch batter, toss them with a little flour instead of cake mix.)

School daze

1 (13×9-inch) cake
1 (19×13-inch) cake board, cut in
  half crosswise and covered, or
  large platter
1½ cups prepared white frosting or
  Buttercream Frosting (page 92)
¾ cup prepared chocolate frosting
  or Chocolate Buttercream
  Frosting (page 93)
2 chocolate sandwich cookies
  Small bear-shaped graham
  cookies
  Assorted color decorator gels
  Assorted candies and fruit rollups
  Black licorice twists

1. Trim top and sides of cake. Using diagram as guide, draw school bus pattern on 13×9-inch piece of waxed paper. Cut pattern out and place on cake. Cut out school bus; place on prepared cake board.

2. Tint white frosting yellow.

3. Frost entire cake with yellow frosting.

4. Frost bottom part of bus with chocolate frosting as shown in photo, reserving small portion for piping. Place 1 chocolate sandwich cookie over each wheel.

5. Using medium writing tip and chocolate frosting, pipe windows and door of bus as shown in photo.

6. Decorate bear-shaped cookies with decorator gels; place cookies in windows and door as shown in photo. Pipe and fill in stop sign with decorator gels. Decorate bus with candies and licorice as shown in photo. *Makes 12 to 16 servings*

Diagram

9½"

13"

9"

cake tip

If you're not very experienced with piping frosting, you may want to draw the windows and the door on the bus with a wooden toothpick before piping. Having lines to follow will make the job easier (and less messy).

school daze

Slam dunk

1 (9-inch) round cake
1 (12-inch) round cake board,
covered, or large plate
1¾ cups prepared white frosting or
Buttercream Frosting (page 92)
3 to 4 black licorice twists
Small clean sponge

1. Trim top and side of cake. Place on prepared cake board.

2. Reserve ¼ cup frosting. Tint 1¼ cups frosting deep orange (rust) and remaining ¼ cup frosting black.

3. Frost entire cake with orange frosting.

4. Place licorice twists end to end around edge of cake to create rim of basketball hoop, trimming licorice as needed. Chill cake 15 minutes to set.

5. Press very slightly dampened clean sponge against top and side of cake, to create dimpled surface resembling texture of basketball.

6. Using medium writing tip and black frosting, pipe line design on top of cake. Pipe net design on side of cake with reserved white frosting as shown in photo.　　*Makes 10 to 12 servings*

cake tips

Cake layers, whether prepared from a mix or from scratch, should rest about 15 minutes in the pans on a cooling rack before being removed from the pans. After 15 minutes or so, what you used to grease the pan will set up, and the cake may stick to the pan. If you try to turn the cake out of the pan in much less than 15 minutes, the hot cake may split. Larger cakes, such as bundt and 13×9-inch cakes, should rest a little longer (about 20 minutes) before they are removed from the pans.

Remember that layer cakes and 13×9-inch cakes must be flipped back over once they are turned out of the pans—these cakes should cool top sides up on wire racks. Bundt cakes, however, only need to be turned out of the pans and left to cool with their fluted edges up.

Slinky the Snake

2 (10-inch) bundt cakes
1 (40×20-inch) cake board, covered
2 cans (16 ounces each) white
    frosting
1 cup semisweet chocolate chips
    Red fruit rollup
    Assorted candies

1. Cut each bundt cake in half. Position cake halves end to end to form one long serpentine shape as shown in photo. Place on prepared cake board, attaching pieces with small amount of frosting.

2. Tint frosting lime green.

3. Frost entire length of cake with green frosting, spreading frosting about halfway down sides of cake.

4. Place chocolate chips in small plastic food storage bag. Microwave on MEDIUM (50% power) 20 seconds. Knead bag several times, then microwave 20 seconds more on medium until chocolate is melted. Cut small tip off one corner of bag; pipe diamond pattern on back of snake as shown in photo.

5. Cut out tongue shape from fruit rollup; attach to snake's head. Decorate face and back of snake with assorted candies.   *Makes 32 to 36 servings*

cake tips

Dusting the inside of a cake pan with flour helps the cake develop a thin, crisp, easily frosted crust and also prevents the cake from absorbing the fat used to grease the pan. Use all-purpose flour, sprinkling about 1 tablespoon into the pan and then shaking and tilting the pan until the bottom and sides have a fine coating. Hold the pan upside down over the sink and tap it gently on the side so any excess flour falls away.

If you're baking a chocolate cake, dust the pan with unsweetened cocoa powder instead of flour to give the cake a more intense chocolate flavor.

speedy the turtle

5½ cups cake batter, divided
1 (10-inch) round cake board, covered, or large plate
1¼ cups prepared white frosting or Buttercream Frosting (page 92)
5 to 6 pecan swirl rolls
Assorted candies and red licorice whip
4 walnut halves

1. Preheat oven to 350°F. Grease and flour 2½-quart ovenproof bowl and medium muffin pan. Pour 4 cups cake batter into prepared bowl; pour remaining cake batter into muffin pan (¼ cup batter per muffin cup). Bake cake in bowl 60 to 70 minutes and cupcakes about 20 minutes or until wooden skewer inserted into centers comes out clean. Cool 15 minutes in pans. Loosen edges; invert onto wire racks and cool completely.

2. Trim flat side of bowl cake. Place on prepared cake board, flat side down. Cut about one-third off bottom of one cupcake. (Reserve remaining cupcakes for another use.)

3. Tint frosting green.

4. Frost cake and cupcake with green frosting. Attach cupcake to cake with small amount of frosting to form turtle head as shown in photo.

5. Cut pecan swirl rolls into ¼-inch-thick slices. Place pecan swirl slices close together to form rows until entire body of turtle is covered. Press candy into center of each pecan roll slice.

6. Decorate face with assorted candies and licorice; arrange walnut halves, flat sides down, to resemble feet as shown in photo. *Makes 14 to 18 servings*

cake tip

To prevent the cake from moving around while you are frosting and decorating it, place a small amount of frosting in the center of the cake board or platter before setting the cake down on it. This will secure the cake to the cake board and can be done with cakes of any size or shape.

Stegosaurus Steve

1 (13×9-inch) cake
1 (19×13-inch) cake board, cut in
   half crosswise and covered, or
   large platter
2¼ cups prepared white frosting or
   Buttercream Frosting (page 92)
Assorted hard candies and
   gumdrops

1. Trim top and sides of cake. Using Diagram 1 as guide, draw stegosaurus pattern on 13×9-inch piece of waxed paper. Cut pattern out and place on cake. Cut out stegosaurus; place on prepared cake board. Attach piece B to piece A using small amount of frosting as shown in Diagram 2.

2. Reserve ¼ cup frosting. Tint remaining frosting dark purple.

3. Frost entire cake with purple frosting.

4. Using medium writing tip and reserved white frosting, pipe outline of stegosaurus and body parts as shown in photo.

5. Decorate stegosaurus with candies as shown in photo.

Makes 12 to 16 servings

Diagram 1

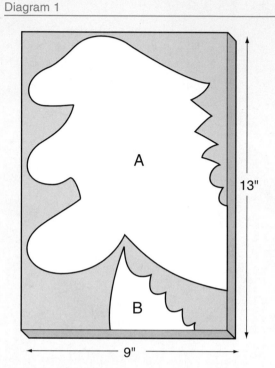

13"

9"

Diagram 2

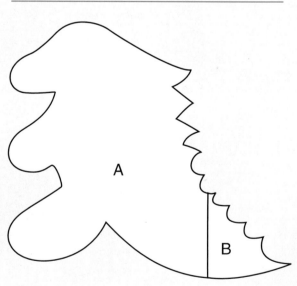

stegosaurus steve

Stripes

5½ cups cake batter, divided
1 (10-inch) round cake board, covered, or large platter
1 can (16 ounces) white frosting
3 chocolate sandwich cookies
1 individual chocolate-covered cake roll
Pretzel sticks
Chocolate sprinkles
Assorted candies and red licorice whip

1. Preheat oven to 350°F. Grease and flour 9-inch round cake pan and medium muffin pan. Pour 3½ cups cake batter into cake pan; pour remaining cake batter into muffin pan (¼ cup batter per muffin cup). Bake cake in pan 35 to 45 minutes and cupcakes about 20 minutes or until toothpick inserted into centers comes out clean. Cool 15 minutes in pans. Loosen edges; invert onto wire racks and cool completely.

2. Trim tops and sides of round cake and two cupcakes. (Reserve remaining cupcakes for another use.) Place cake on prepared cake board. Position two cupcakes next to cake to form ears.

3. Tint frosting orange.

4. Frost entire cake and cupcakes with orange frosting.

5. Carefully open two sandwich cookies to expose white filling. Place opened cookies on tiger's ears. Cut two thin slices from cake roll; place on tiger's face for eyes.

6. Add pretzel whiskers, cookie nose, candy mouth and chocolate sprinkle stripes as shown in photo.

Makes 12 to 14 servings

cake tip
The recipe and basic pattern for this tiger cake can be easily converted to another animal of your choice. If your child prefers bears, lions, leopards or even mice, just change the frosting color and add the appropriate decorations.

touchdown!

1 (13×9-inch) cake
1 (19×13-inch) cake board, cut in
    half crosswise and covered, or
    large platter
2 cups prepared white frosting or
    Buttercream Frosting (page 92)
    Assorted color decorator gels
1 square (2 ounces) almond bark
2 pretzel rods
4 thin pretzel sticks
    Small bear-shaped graham
    cookies

1. Trim top and sides of cake; place on prepared cake board.

2. Tint frosting medium green.

3. Frost entire cake with green frosting. Pipe field lines with white decorator gel.

4. Melt almond bark in tall glass according to package directions. Break off one quarter of each pretzel rod; discard shorter pieces. Break two pretzel sticks in half. Dip pretzels in melted almond bark, turning to coat completely and tapping off excess. Using pretzel rods for support posts, pretzel sticks for crossbars and pretzel stick halves for uprights, arrange pretzels in two goalpost formations on waxed paper; let stand until completely dry. When dry, carefully peel waxed paper from goalposts; place on each end of cake.

5. Meanwhile, decorate bear-shaped cookies with decorator gels; position cookies throughout field as desired.

Makes 16 to 20 servings

cake tip●●●●●●●●●●●●●●●●●●●●●●●●
          It's easy to personalize this football
          field cake—simply choose your
child's favorite colors or teams to decorate the "players". It can be a little difficult and time-consuming to decorate such small cookies, so try starting with dots or blocks of color rather than numbers and shapes.

Where's the fire?

1 (13×9-inch) cake
1 (14×10-inch) cake board, covered
1½ cans (16 ounces each) white frosting
Black licorice twists
Red licorice rope
6 chocolate and vanilla sandwich cookies
Assorted candies

1. Trim top and sides of cake. Cut cake into pieces as shown in Diagram 1.

2. Place piece A on prepared cake board. Place piece B on top of piece A as shown in Diagram 2, attaching pieces with small amount of frosting. Discard piece C.

3. Tint 2 cups frosting red. Frost windshield area with white frosting. Frost remainder of truck with red frosting.

4. Cut licorice twists into pieces; arrange on fire truck to create ladder and bumpers as shown in photo. Arrange licorice rope on top of truck to resemble hose.

5. Position sandwich cookies for wheels. Decorate fire truck with assorted candies as shown in photo.

Makes 16 to 18 servings

Diagram 1

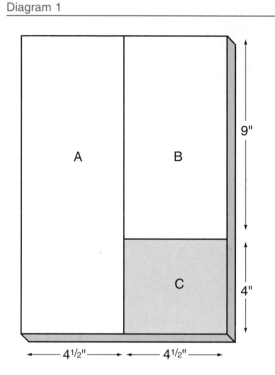

Diagram 2

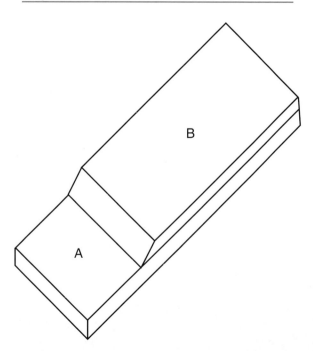

Your Move

1 (9-inch) square cake
1 (10-inch) square cake board,
    covered, or large platter
1 cup prepared white frosting or
    Buttercream Frosting (page 92)
15 square dark chocolate mints
8 to 10 chocolate candies
8 to 10 chocolate and white
    chocolate candies

1. Trim top and sides of cake.

2. Frost entire cake with white frosting.

3. Place square chocolate mints in checkerboard pattern on top of cake as shown in photo.

4. Arrange candies on top of cake as desired. *Makes 10 to 12 servings*

cake tips ●●●●●●●●●●●●●●●●●●●●

When preparing to bake a cake, be sure to have your pans greased and floured before making the batter. Once the batter is poured into the pans, immediately place the pan into a preheated oven. Cake batter should not sit before baking because chemical leaveners begin working as soon as they are mixed with liquids. (However, this is true for scratch cakes but not mix cakes, which do not need to be baked right away.)

Another key to a successful cake is to avoid opening the oven door during the first half of baking time. The oven temperature must remain constant in order for the cake to rise properly.

Zoom!

1 (13×9-inch) cake
2 cans (16 ounces each) white frosting
1 (15×15-inch) cake board, covered, or large platter
4 chocolate sandwich cookies
Assorted candies
Chocolate-covered wafer cookies

1. Trim top of cake. Using Diagram 1 as guide, draw car pattern on 13×9-inch piece of waxed paper. Cut pattern out and place on cake. Cut out car shapes. (Same shape is cut out twice.)

2. Frost one side of car shape lightly with white frosting; press both pieces together and upright on prepared cake board to form race car as shown in Diagram 2.

3. Tint 1 can frosting red. Tint half of remaining can frosting purple.

4. Frost top of car with white frosting to resemble windows. Frost remainder of car and portion of car roof with red frosting as shown in photo.

5. Using medium writing tip and purple frosting, pipe numbers and details on car as shown in photo.

6. Position sandwich cookies on sides of car for wheels; decorate car with assorted candies and wafer cookies.

Makes 12 to 14 servings

Diagram 1

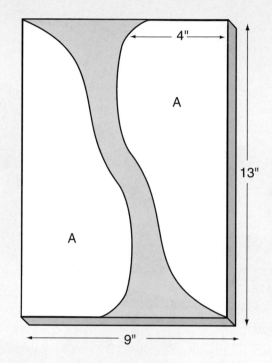

Diagram 2

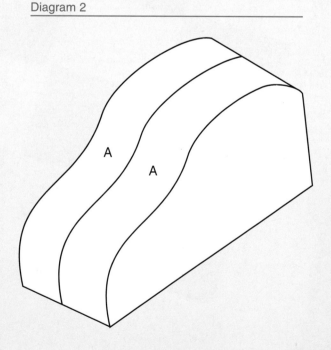

buttercream Frosting

6 cups powdered sugar, sifted, divided
¾ cup butter or margarine, softened
¼ cup shortening
6 to 8 tablespoons milk, divided
1 teaspoon vanilla

Combine 3 cups powdered sugar, butter, shortening, 4 tablespoons milk and vanilla in large bowl. Beat with electric mixer until smooth. Add remaining powdered sugar; beat until light and fluffy, adding more milk, 1 tablespoon at a time, as needed for good spreading consistency.   *Makes about 3½ cups*

Jam Glaze

1 cup apricot or seedless raspberry jam
1 tablespoon water

Bring jam and water to a boil in small saucepan. Remove from heat. Cool before using. Spread over cake and let stand about 1 hour before frosting.
Makes about 1 cup

Note: Use apricot jam if the cake is being covered by a light frosting. The raspberry jam is particularly good with chocolate cake and frosting.

Tip: Jam Glaze can be used instead of a base frosting to help seal in crumbs and add extra flavor.

Chocolate buttercream frosting

6 cups powdered sugar, sifted,
    divided
1 cup butter or margarine, softened
4 to 6 squares (1 ounce each)
    unsweetened chocolate, melted
    and cooled slightly
8 to 10 tablespoons milk, divided
1 teaspoon vanilla

Combine 3 cups powdered sugar, butter, melted chocolate to taste, 6 tablespoons milk and vanilla in large bowl. Beat with electric mixer until smooth. Add remaining powdered sugar; beat until light and fluffy, adding more milk, 1 tablespoon at a time, as needed for good spreading consistency.

Makes about 3½ cups

Yellow butter Cake

2 cups all-purpose flour
4 teaspoons baking powder
½ teaspoon salt
1½ cups sugar
½ cup butter, softened
1 cup milk
1 teaspoon vanilla
3 eggs

Preheat oven to 350°F. Grease and flour cake pan(s) or grease and line with waxed paper. Sift flour, baking powder and salt together in large bowl. Stir in sugar. Add butter, milk and vanilla; beat with electric mixer at low speed 30 seconds. Beat at medium speed 2 minutes. Add eggs; beat 2 minutes. Pour into prepared cake pan(s) and bake as directed below, until wooden toothpick inserted into center comes out clean.

Cool in pan 10 minutes. Loosen cake edge from pan(s) and invert onto wire rack. Remove waxed paper; cool completely.

Use the following baking times when preparing this cake:

BAKE

★ 1 (13×9-inch) cake: 35 to 40 minutes
★ 1 (10-inch) bundt cake: 45 to 55 minutes
★ 2 (9-inch) rounds: 35 to 40 minutes
★ 2 (8-inch) squares: 30 to 35 minutes
★ 3 (8-inch) rounds: 20 to 25 minutes
★ 8 large (4-inch) cupcakes: 35 to 40 minutes
★ 24 medium (2¾-inch) cupcakes: 20 to 25 minutes

Chocolate Cake

2 cups all-purpose flour
⅔ cup unsweetened cocoa powder
1¾ teaspoons baking soda
½ teaspoon baking powder
½ teaspoon salt
1¾ cups sugar
⅔ cup shortening
1 cup cold water
2 teaspoons vanilla
3 eggs

Preheat oven to 350°F. Grease and flour cake pan(s) or grease and line with waxed paper. Sift flour, cocoa, baking soda, baking powder and salt together in large bowl. Stir in sugar. Add shortening. Gradually beat in water at low speed with electric mixer until combined. Stir in vanilla. Beat at high speed 2 minutes. Add eggs; beat 2 minutes. Pour into prepared cake pan(s) and bake as directed below, until wooden toothpick inserted into center comes out clean. Cool in pan 10 minutes. Loosen cake edge from pan(s) and invert onto wire rack. Remove waxed paper; cool completely.

Use the following baking times when preparing this cake:

To save time: Bake cakes ahead of time and store them until you are ready to decorate. If you will be using the cake layers within the next two days, wrap them tightly in foil or plastic wrap and store in a cool place, but not the refrigerator. For longer storage, freeze cakes wrapped in heavy-duty foil or stored in airtight freezer bags. Cakes will keep frozen for up to two months. Thaw frozen cakes, unwrapped, at room temperature.

Decorated cakes can also be stored for up to one month. Freeze the unwrapped, frosted cake for 1 to 2 hours or until the frosting has hardened. Then wrap tightly in heavy-duty foil and store in the freezer. Unwrap a decorated cake before thawing.

BAKE

★ 1 (13×9-inch) cake: 35 to 40 minutes

★ 1 (10-inch) bundt cake: 45 to 55 minutes

★ 2 (9-inch) rounds: 35 to 40 minutes

★ 2 (8-inch) squares: 30 to 35 minutes

★ 3 (8-inch) rounds: 20 to 25 minutes

★ 8 large (4-inch) cupcakes: 35 to 40 minutes

★ 24 medium (2¾-inch) cupcakes: 20 to 25 minutes